M000198276

A GIFT FOR

_____

THANKS
FOR ALL
YOU DO

Published by Sellers Publishing, Inc.
161 John Roberts Road, South Portland, ME 04106
Visit us at www.sellerspublishing.com • E-mail: rsp@rsvp.com

Copyright © 2015 Sellers Publishing, Inc.

Images copyright © 2015 Shutterstock

All rights reserved.

ISBN-13: 978-1-4162-4547-6

Printed and bound in China.

10 9 8 7 6 5 4 3 2 1

THANKS
FOR ALL YOU DO

ROBIN HAYWOOD

SELLERS

PUBLISHING

Thanks
for
being
awesome!

You have the ability to see sunny skies where others see only cloudy days.

You deserve
a big hand
for all your
good work.

You are the reason
we stand strong.

Your personal
commitment to
quality is obvious
in everything
you do.

You've
got a
winner's
attitude!

Your generous
nature makes
all the difference.

We sincerely hope that you will continue to stay in our organization; we have big plans for you!

All achievements begin with an idea. Your innovations put those ideas front and center. Thank you.

Your perspective on
"what is really important"
inspires all of us.
Thank you for
suggesting we stop
"and smell the roses."

Not everyone is a creative thinker, but you are.

You make it
look so easy!

You're a real smarty pants at your job!

Thanks for keeping us all on our toes.

I can always spot
you in a crowd –
your work
stands out!

It's a pleasure to work with you – thanks for all you do.

We can always
count on you
in a crunch.

You help us
stand tall!

Thanks
for not taking
the shortcut.

You nailed it!
Your effort
hit the mark.

We appreciate
your flexibility in
tough situations.